Given with love and laughter to

___Aimee___

from

___Paula___

Motherhood
A Celebration of Blessings & Blunders

Nancy Moser

Harold Shaw Publishers
Wheaton, Illinois

Copyright © 1997 by Nancy Moser

All rights reserved. No part of this book may be reproduced or transmitted in any form or by any means, electronic or mechanical, including photocopying, recording, or any information storage and retrieval system without written permission from Harold Shaw Publishers, Box 567, Wheaton, Illinois, 60189. Printed in the United States of America.

All Scripture quotations, unless otherwise indicated, are taken from the HOLY BIBLE, NEW INTERNATIONAL VERSION®. NIV®. Copyright © 1973, 1978, 1984 International Bible Society. Used by permission of Zondervan Publishing House. All rights reserved.

ISBN 0-87788-564-8

Cover design by David LaPlaca

Library of Congress Cataloging-in-Publication Data applied for

05 04 03 02 01 00 99 98 97

10 9 8 7 6 5 4 3 2 1

To my blessed children: Emily, Carson and Laurel.
Forgive my faults and remember me fondly.

Ready or Not, Here Comes Motherhood!

"Faith is being sure of what we hope for and certain of what we do not see." Hebrews 11:1

"I can't do this!"

I've said those words many times throughout my life—but never with more conviction than when I was pregnant with each of our three children.

You know the scenario. The baby you're carrying takes as many steps as you do throughout the day, jabbing you with tiny knees and elbows. You become obsessed with the thought of eating something full of additives, caffeine and fat. And if your husband tells you you're beautiful one more time (keeping his eyes handily focused above shoulder level), you will start acting as ugly as you feel.

That's when those four little words start popping into your consciousness, sneaking up on you, interrupting whatever thirty seconds of calm you may have been enjoying—a little like a special bulletin on TV or a tornado siren cutting through the summer night.

It's the moment you realize the only way out of your pregnant situation is pain. And it scares you.

Pregnancy is like getting on a roller coaster, strapping yourself in and feeling the car begin to roll. No matter how flat the track at the beginning, no matter how slow and steady the climb, you *know* a screaming, stomach-wrenching thrill awaits you at the top.

Adoptive moms can also ride the roller coaster of worry. Their fears can be even deeper and more debilitating. At least a mother giving birth knows a general time frame for the event. Often, an adoptive mom must suffer through the agony of "when" or even worse, "if."

But all this is worth it when your baby is placed in your arms for the first time. All the pain, the waiting, the worries, the fear dissolve before the miracle of this new life.

God's way is wondrous. We may tell him "I can't" but luckily he doesn't listen. In fact, often the truly amazing moments in life are created when we think we can't do something. That's when we have to pull ourselves together, put our faith in him and get out of his way.

That's when miracles happen. Like motherhood.

It Goes Without Saying

> *"For these commands are a lamp, this teaching is a light,
> and the corrections of discipline are the way to life."*
> Proverbs 6:23

Mothers and children share a special telepathy. Within weeks of her baby's birth, a new mother will be able to tell whether her baby is crying because he wants a human link, a bottle to drink or because his bottom stinks. The tiniest peep in the middle of the night will send a mother running to her child's crib.

As the years go by, these telepathic skills become finely honed. When an older child yells, "Mom!" from the backyard, a mother can return to balancing the checkbook in a matter of seconds, having determined the outburst was caused by a sharing dispute and not the infliction of bodily harm.

Inflection is a vital factor in this communication. When I ask my kids if their rooms are clean, I can tell by their slight hesitation and the rise of their voices at the end of "Uh-huh," that they aren't being entirely truthful. And only a mother can say a child's name and have it represent a dozen emotions spanning elation to doom.

Not all this telepathy is extrasensory. They say that when one sense is weak, the others kick in. And since we mothers' common sense is weakened due to an overabundance of laundry and a shortage of privacy, our other five senses go on double duty. Consider the sense of hearing. How many teenagers can get past a mother-sentry whose ears are fine-tuned to each creak in the stairs and the click of the back door versus the front? None.

Then there is body language. When my children were younger, I would hear a bump from upstairs and yell out a general, "Kids! What's going on? Come down here!" I could tell the extent of their mischief-making by how far they came into the room. The most guilty stood in the hallway. Co-conspirators leaned on the door jamb. And those who were innocent (or the best liars) sat on my lap. And what child has not perfected the art of knowing when to ask for an extra dollar by reading their mother's body language?

Yet beyond all this is a glow, a light that can be felt, a light that will not be dimmed no matter how many broken vases, muddy shoes and harsh words clatter between mother and child through the years. That light is a gift from God—the light of love.

Sorting Out the Pieces

"Teach me to do your will, for you are my God;
may your good Spirit lead me on level ground."
Psalm 143:10

There is one particular toy owned by every toddler in America. I believe ownership of this toy is a requirement before the child turns two. It's the shape box. A child matches the shaped piece with the hole in the box. Then she picks up the box and shakes it until her mother shrieks from mental collapse. Then she starts all over again.

The shape box teaches hand-eye coordination, matching, the names of colors and geometric shapes (can you say "trapezoid"?). And by watching my oldest daughter, Emily, master this toy as a toddler, I learned a lesson myself.

When she first got the shape box—actually a ball—Emily sat in the middle of the living room and proceeded to do what all children do instinctively: dump the pieces as noisily as possible. I sat beside her to help, but as she scooted away it was clear she wanted to do it herself.

Emily picked up a yellow square and pushed it against a triangular opening. She cocked the piece to the side. It still wouldn't go. Turning the ball, she tried over and over in the hole for the oval, the circle, the octagon, the rectangle. It took great motherly restraint not to point at the square opening and say, "It goes in here."

Unfortunately, Emily would never find the right opening because she was holding the ball with her fingers through that very hole. I tried to take the ball and show her, but she held it tight. "Mine!" she said.

Finally she surrendered, tossed it aside and pouted. *Don't give up!* I handed her the square piece and pointed to the correct hole. When Emily pushed the shape through, her face glowed in triumph.

Like Emily forcing her will on her toy, I have tried to force my will on life and on God. He's given me all the right pieces of life, with very specific places they should go. But how often have I held on too tightly, intent on doing things my way—until I fail, throw things aside and pout? How many times has he waited patiently, allowing me these failures even though he could have easily prevented them? Finally, when I admit defeat and surrender to him, he hands me my life and asks me to start over again. Only then—if I let him guide me—does everything fit.

Storage Bins, Cat Races and Lace

"I wish that all men were as I am. But each man has his own gift from God; one has this gift, another has that." 1 Corinthians 7:7

Where did my children come from?

Oh, I know *that*. I was there at the time. But how did my three children, whom I bore in the same city, in the same family, within one decade, turn out so incredibly different from each other?

The oldest, Emily, is an organizer. Give her some plastic storage bins, shelf dividers and drawer trays and she's occupied for days. She's off to college now—an act of independence she's been waiting for since she was twelve. She will tolerate no frills on her clothes and will not wear a solid red shirt with solid blue pants even though they complement each other. "They don't match," she says. She works twenty hours a week and gets good grades with little effort. Ask her if she needs help and she'll reply, "No, I can handle it." And, usually, she can.

Our only boy, Carson, is the sensitive one. I can always count on Carson to notice a new haircut or dress. Animals flock to him; he has races with our cats and has taught them to fetch. If he is watching TV, don't talk to him because he won't hear you. He'll "forget" to do his chores, yet he'll work harder than any man if you assign him a special project. Occasionally he trips on air, yet he can hit a grand slam like a pro.

Within a half hour, our youngest, Laurel, will say goodnight three times with varying degrees of pathos and hugs. At age four she could perform "America" from "West Side Story" with gusto. If you ask her to bring her shoes to her room, they will get as far as the hall outside. At age eleven she has planned her wedding a dozen times, with the most lacy, ruffly dresses getting top billing. When there are chores to be done, her arm or leg starts hurting and within minutes of getting into trouble, she's at your side saying, "I need a hug."

Why are they so different?

There is only one explanation: the characteristics of our children come from God. "Before I formed you in the womb I knew you, before you were born I set you apart" (Jeremiah 1:5).

My children are his, and I must let them go his way. What could be more exciting than watching each of them learn that his way can be their way?

The Consequence of Toddler Radar

"If a man will not work, he shall not eat." 2 Thessalonians 3:10

We were at my parents' Colorado cabin exactly three minutes when it happened—an event that determined our days and evenings for the coming week.

During those fateful three minutes, Laurel (who was two at the time) found the toy shelves with a radar perfected by toddlers. Did she pull out the dominoes, playing cards, or coloring books? Nope. She found the puzzles and promptly dumped them on the floor. Not simple kid puzzles of Big Bird or Mickey Mouse, but complicated grown-up puzzles of red barns, mountain vistas and French cafes. Three thousand puzzle pieces lay on the floor where Laurel gleefully mixed them together.

Although working puzzles during the chilly mountain evenings was often a favorite pastime of ours, being forced to reinvent three puzzles whose skies matched was not looked upon with willing hearts.

"Come on, guys, this will be fun," I said.

Carson and Emily gave me the appropriate "Mom, you're crazy" look. My husband, Mark, found sudden interest in a decorating magazine.

"Me, Mommy. Me!" Laurel said, climbing onto a chair by the puzzle table. I led her to the coloring books, reminding her that she'd had her chance and at this point it was best she keep her sweet little mitts occupied elsewhere.

Then I transferred a handful of pieces to the table and began turning them right-side up. One, two . . . two thousand two hundred twenty-two. "I need some help here," I said.

"But I want to play Barbies," Emily said.

"Me too," Carson said (he usually tortured Barbies).

"I get the one with the prom dress," Mark said.

A piece of divine wisdom sprang to mind. "Those who don't work don't eat," I said. Three sets of eyes dared me.

"Okay, I'll revise that," I said. "Those who don't work don't get s'mores tonight."

Four sets of hands turned over puzzle pieces. Actually, five sets of hands. I always was a sucker for the puppy eyes of a two-year-old.

Besides, Laurel deserved it. We had her to thank for those long evenings spent together. Laurel—and the enticement of chocolate with gooey marshmallows.

Spicy Snakes and Sugary Snails

"Know that the LORD is God.
It is he who made us, and we are his."
Psalm 100:3

Before I had children I wondered at the rhyme about little girls being made of "sugar and spice and everything nice" and boys being made of "snakes and snails and puppy dog tails." How could anyone make such blanket statements about males and females? Now, as a mother, I see the wisdom of that unknown poet.

There must be a gene in little girls that makes them want to wear their mother's shoes—the higher the heel and the closer to the stairs the better. I never once suggested to my daughters, "Come on, sweetie, I want you to try on Mommy's shoes." Or necklaces, or lipstick, or belts (wrapped three times around). *Why are they this way?*

There is a corresponding gene in little boys that makes them not care if their nose is running. This trait begins as a toddler but doesn't completely disappear until the boy is . . . it never completely disappears. Ever. *Why are they this way?*

And only girls roll their eyes at boys, declaring with this one gesture that they (the girls) are above and beyond the male species. Have you ever seen a boy roll his eyes at a girl? Never.

Consider the friendships between girl children. The intricacies of Mideast diplomacy are not as tangled as the negotiations, counteractions and introspections that go on between "best friends" of the female persuasion. Yet boys can smack each other in the eye, call each other names and be sharing a Popsicle in the span of ten minutes with no indication that blood was spilled only moments before. *Why are they this way?*

Because it's God's way. It is he who made us and we are his. What a boring world this would be if we were all the same. How handy it is that Mark is one way and I'm another and there's someone to clean the toilet and someone else to fix it when it overflows; that the scraped knees of fatherly horseplay can be cared for with a Band-Aid and a motherly kiss. Instead of fighting the differences in each other, we should celebrate them.

Trust him. God knew what he was doing.

Oops

"I will instruct you and teach you in the way you should go;
I will counsel you and watch over you."
Psalm 32:8

News bulletin: parents aren't perfect. I am the living, breathing, often-defective proof. I make mistakes. Bushels of them.

When our daughter, Emily, was a year old, I worked mornings outside the home. On the way to work I took her to a babysitter a few blocks away. Mornings were rushed with the logistics of getting dressed and fed. It was during this rush that I made this particular booboo—although I would not find out about it until later.

After work, I picked up Emily from the sitter's and brought her home. We had some lunch and I put her down for a nap. That's when I discovered my mistake. When I took off Emily's rubber-toed tennis shoes, I noticed the toes seemed stiff. Looking inside the shoes, I found a pair of socks, stuffed into the toes. Emily had worn the shoes all morning with her little toes crammed against yesterday's socks!

This, of course, is not the kind of incident that scars children for life. But I have made other, more serious errors in raising our three children. My list of motherly mistakes rivals my grocery list during two-for-one specials. I can't remember how many times I was too strict—or too lenient. Or times when I should have apologized—and didn't. I try to forget the times I escaped to the bathroom to cry because I was ashamed or because I had absolutely no idea what to do.

But I never gave up. Right or wrong, I loved my kids enough to make a decision. The words "I don't care" crossed my mind but never my lips.

If only we could touch a piece of God's perfection, experience a moment of his perfect wisdom. He doesn't make mistakes. Through every crisis we create or every pitfall we pinpoint, we take comfort in knowing he is with us, helping us, guiding us. Perhaps in the larger scheme of things, our mistakes aren't mistakes at all—they are God's perfect way of teaching us as we teach our children.

We care about our children enough to make mistakes. How wonderful that God cares for us in spite of them.

When Silence Shouts

*"O LORD, you have searched me and you know me.
You know when I sit and when I rise,
you perceive my thoughts from afar." Psalm 139:1-2*

It was too quiet.

With three kids, silence shouts. It's deafening.

Only minutes before they'd been in my face, talking, arguing, overwhelming me with their energy as I sorted my husband's socks. With their help, the completion of my chore stretched into the next millennium. I shooed them out of the room, adding the most regrettable words a parent will ever say: "Go find something to do." Saying that was like giving a burglar the key to our house, giving my husband the remote control, or putting a Snickers bar within my arm's reach.

The first clue I had that something was amiss was the silence that wove its way through our home. First, there was noise, then there wasn't. I held my breath and pricked up my ears, sensing danger. No television. No music. No conversations. Not even a toilet flushing in the deep recesses of the house. I rolled a black and a navy sock together for safekeeping and ventured out of the bedroom. I tiptoed, hoping my breathing wouldn't give me away. I hugged the wall like a commando on an enemy reconnaissance.

A thump from the kitchen. I stopped, my heart racing. A giggle. A "Shhh!" Time for the offensive. Straightening my shoulders, I strode into the kitchen. "What's going on—"

No one was there. *How silly I was to suspect—*

Six hazel eyes appeared over the top of the cooking island. Three mouths shaped the word "Uh-oh." A pan of brownies was accidentally kicked into view.

I assumed the General Mom position: hands on hips, eyes stern with a wrinkle etching its way between my brows. "Don't you remember me telling you no more brownies?"

Emily, the leader of the Moser gang, spoke up. "You told us no brownies ages ago. We didn't think it meant now."

I picked up the pan. "It means now. It means no brownies until I tell you different. Go get a game and set it up on the kitchen table. I'll be back in a few minutes."

I returned to the bedroom to finish the socks. As I sorted, I thought of the uncertainty of silence. Sometimes silence means we're pensive, thoughtful, waiting. Other times it shouts with deception or builds a wall. I thought of what God does when he finds us silent with scheming—when our silence shouts. Although he doesn't slink along the walls we've erected or tiptoe down the hall to our hiding place, I could imagine him holding his breath just like I'd done, a little sorrowful that he's been forced to chastise us.

I closed the dresser drawer and headed back to the noises in the kitchen: the click of tossed dice, the scrape of chair against floor, voices counting "one, two, three." I put the pan of brownies away and I watched, laughed and listened to the sounds of my children—as God did the same from his heavenly perch.

Who's the Boss?

*"Come, my children, listen to me;
I will teach you the fear of the LORD."
Psalm 34:11*

When Emily was in second grade she brought home a note from school. Apparently Emily thought she could do better than the teacher. Her attempt at a coup was not looked upon kindly.

I was not surprised by the teacher's note. Emily was a typical oldest child, a leader. With each new sibling she assumed the babies were brought home for her to mother, love and command.

After reading the note to Emily, we sat on the floor for a chat. Knowing the power of visual aids, I collected all the Fisher-Price Little People. "These are the kids in your class," I said, lining the people up at invisible desks. I held up a girl in a red dress. "This is you," I said. "And this is your teacher." I held up a grandmother-type with a bun and glasses.

"My teacher doesn't have glasses. And I don't have a red dress," Emily said.

I closed my eyes and prayed for patience. "Just pretend, okay?" Next question. "Where does the teacher belong?" I asked.

Emily thought a moment, then got a plastic desk from the toy box. "The teacher goes up here, by the desk."

"Very good," I said.

Now for the clincher. I held up the "Emily" toy. "What would happen if a student went to the front of the class next to the teacher and said, 'Look at me! I'm in charge now'?"

"They can't do that. The teacher wouldn't like it."

Gotcha!

"But that's what you're doing when you try to act like the teacher," I said. "It's like standing in front of the whole class and saying, 'Look at me! I'm in charge now.' "

Emily put the red-dressed student back in its place with the rest of the class. She nodded, resigned to the humble chore of surrendering to authority. . . .

Emily's not the only one who has trouble relinquishing control. Every day I struggle with wanting to be in charge, thinking I can do it better than anyone else. Many times God has had to set me gently in my place. I need to remember to look at *him. He's* in charge. Now and forever.

Move over, Emily. Save me a seat.

God in the Details

> *"I kneel before the Father, from whom his whole family in heaven and on earth derives its name." Ephesians 3:14-15*

Everyone in my family knows a lot about the others' habits and idiosyncrasies. We know where each of us will sit when we pile in the van, we know where each of us will shuck off our shoes when we're relaxing at home, we know what each of us will order in our favorite restaurants.

Well, almost. Mark suffers from fast-food amnesia. There is no explaining this phenomenon. I can't even pass it off as a man thing. And it certainly has no relation to his intelligence, since Mark knows at least as much as the rest of us know, if not a few pages more. But every time we visit a fast-food restaurant it happens. As we're standing in line, we remind Mark what we want to eat and he nods as if he has filed the information into a safe place. One of the kids stays with him to help carry the trays, while the rest of us disperse to the dining area.

This is when the inevitable happens. Sparked by the words "May I help you?" Mark's memory is completely erased. At this point he looks to the child beside him and asks, "What did they want?"

Yet with the exception of Mark's visits into la-la land, each of us *does* know what the others want, down to the side of ranch dressing for my chimichanga and the "hold the tomatoes" on Carson's taco salad; down to the mustard for Mark, the curly fries for Emily and the "suicide" drink for Laurel (a squirt of all the soda flavors mixed together).

But this family knowledge goes beyond the frivolities of favorite foods and shucked-off shoes. It delves deep into the cores of our personalities. Only by experiencing the caring of a family do I know that when Laurel's eyes light up and she bounces on her toes she is thinking (if not saying) she's so happy she'd like to do cartwheels. Only by experiencing the love of a family do we know by the sound of Mark's briefcase on the counter what kind of day he had at work. Only by sharing the experiences of a family do my kids know that when I flick a wrist at them while I'm at the computer it means, "Just a second, I've got an idea rolling."

So it is with God. As we grow closer to him, the things that count the most are not only the big blessings he gives, but the small things he knows, the details that show his caring, his love and his sharing the experiences of our lives.

Those tiny details prove we are indeed creatures of habit. We're in the habit of being a family—with God as the head. How lucky we are that it's a habit we never have to break.

Onions and Other Experiments

*"Let the wise listen and add to their learning,
and let the discerning get guidance."*
Proverbs 1:5

No one who knows me would ever believe this, but I am a gourmet cook at heart.

At heart, I said, not in reality. That's only because my family doesn't allow me to be a gourmet cook. It's all their fault.

I've experienced a few spells of chef-dom, where I've actually perused a cookbook for fun, been seduced by the full-color pictures, and decided to create a culinary masterpiece. I've gone to the grocery store and bought things like cilantro, white pepper and hoisin sauce. I've come home, inspired. I've cleared the kitchen counter of yesterday's paper, today's mail and tomorrow's bills. I've set any stray child in a chair a safe distance away and dug out the avocado gingham apron I made in 4-H when I was twelve.

"Whatcha makin'?" one brave child would invariably ask.

"A feast."

"Are those onions? I don't like onions."

"Yes, those are onions."

"Are those green peppers?" child #2 would pipe up. "I don't like green peppers."

"Yes, those are green peppers."

"Are those mushrooms?" child #3 would ask. "I don't like—"

"YES, they are mushrooms," I tell them. "And I don't care if you like them!"

This story illustrates the main reason I am not a gourmet cook. In order to attain this distinction you have to use ingredients that don't come from a box or a can. Unfortunately, such exotic ingredients as onions are not fully appreciated by my family, Mark included. After picking onions out of whatever I cook, they accuse me of using them as guinea pigs. Imagine.

If only they would be brave and let me show them what I can do. But they're so set in their ways that they don't—

Hmm. Funny how so many lessons I'd like my family to learn sound like something I'm supposed to learn myself. Maybe that's why God made us mothers, so we could learn by osmosis. . . .

What I said about my family, God could say to me: *If only she would be brave and let me show her what I can do. But she is so set in her ways that she won't—*

Imagine.

Eluding the Perfection Police

"There, in the presence of the LORD your God, you and your families shall eat and shall rejoice in everything you have put your hand to, because the LORD your God has blessed you." Deuteronomy 12:7

I am not the best housekeeper. There are dust bunnies in my house I've made into pets. I see no reason to vacuum the carpet just to remove footprints. And I know for a fact that a few waterspots on my kitchen faucet will not spread plague germs throughout our home.

It's not that I don't know how to be a perfect Suzy Homemaker. Hey, I watch Donna Reed reruns. Yet after twenty-one years of marriage, three kids, three cats and five houses, I have determined—and chosen—to take it down a notch.

When the imaginary perfection police used to invade my domain, I would bark orders: "Carson, you cut a swath through the family room. Emily, hose down the kitchen and Laurel, capture all the dust bunnies. I'll conquer the laundry. Any questions?"

Carson raised a hand. "Why are we doing this?" he asked. "Is Grandma coming to visit?"

"No."

"The Pope?"

I glared at them. "No one's coming to visit. We're cleaning the house for *us*. We *do* like a clean house, don't we?"

Realizing this was a trick question, the kids looked at each other and shrugged.

"What's that shrug supposed to mean?" I snapped.

"We'll help," Emily said, "but we don't understand why you're so . . . so . . ."

"Zealous," Carson said.

We all stared at him. "Where did you get that word?" I asked.

Carson looked at the ceiling, trying to remember. "I think I read it in the newspaper in an article about wild-eyed fanatics who tried to take over—"

"Are you implying I'm a fanatic?" I asked, brandishing a broom in the air like a sword.

My children's silence was my answer. I looked around the room at the morning newspaper strewn on the coffee table, a lone pair of shoes by the wall, the couch pillows which would only take a few moments to straighten.

"Maybe I was exaggerating a bit," I conceded. "Maybe things aren't as messy as I thought."

The kids' shoulders relaxed. They'd been given a reprieve from the perfection police—and their zealous mother.

The perfection police visit far less often now. The popcorn bowl in the sink, mail on the counter and a baseball hat flung over the stair post are not capital crimes. They're proof that a family lives here.

That is true perfection.

Do Not Enter

"Come to me, all you who are weary and burdened, and I will give you rest." Matthew 11:28

Years ago when the kids were small we lived in a different house. In that house was my "dream room," a library I preferred to keep child-free. The room had oak paneling on the walls *and* ceiling, as well as built-in shelves for my books and knickknacks (otherwise known as "no-nos"). We didn't exactly erect barricades around the library, but the kids knew they'd best have a really good reason to be in there.

The library was also the sanctuary where I began my writing career, working on a computer that dated from the Cro-Magnon era of technology. It had 20 megabytes of memory and used disks that were truly floppy. The background of the screen was gray and the words were a sickly shade of green. One of my biggest fears was that the kids (or I) would push a wrong button and my literary masterpiece would be lost in MS-DOS oblivion. When I caught two-year-old Laurel studying one of my floppy disks (her intentions were *not* honorable), I saved it with the same sort of heroic zeal you see on episodes of "Rescue 911." If I could have erected a force field to keep my kids a safe distance from my territory, I would have.

Of course, now things are different. We've moved, floppy disks are hard, the memory bytes of the computer exceed the zeros in the national debt, and the old gray monitor looks more like a color TV. If I have trouble on my new computer, it talks to me, telling me what's wrong—or I'll call in the kids, begging them for their expertise.

It's better this way. No barricades, no imaginary force fields. The kids and I can share our knowledge, our time, our space.

Unfortunately there are other barriers I haven't pulled down, emotional and spiritual rooms I prefer to keep closed off from my family and from God. I know it would be best if I opened these rooms and let him in, if I gave him free rein to rearrange, to touch, to organize these private spaces of my life. But it's hard. I need to let down the barricades guarding those corners of my life and let God in. Only then can I truly share my life—all of it—with him, as he desires.

Like I Always Say . . .

*"Train a child in the way he should go,
and when he is old he will not turn from it."*
Proverbs 22:6

As a mother, I always have the feeling nobody's listening. I'm wrong.

Let me back up. Every summer we try to arrange it so at least one of our kids can spend a week with the grandparents up in Lincoln, Nebraska. But as the kids get older and busier, it gets harder. This last year, only Laurel was able to go.

I do more than approve of these visits; I encourage the intergenerational bonding. I especially like it because my mom teaches Laurel all the things I don't have time to teach her. At my parents' house, Laurel goes golfing (she loves washing the golf balls) and to Bible study (where she's the youngest by a good fifty years). She bakes cookies and embroiders pillowcases.

At my mother-in-law's house, Laurel plays dress-up in a stash of Bev's Sarah Coventry jewelry. She learns how to make pan-fried chicken and how to fold laundry so it becomes an art form. (Can I come along next year?)

It was at Bev's house that Laurel revealed that *I* had actually taught her something.

Laurel's younger cousin Brittney stayed over one night, giving Grandma two giggling girls to contend with. The next morning, in usual grandma fashion, Bev told the girls, "You can have whatever you want for breakfast."

Visions of sugarplums! Powdered doughnuts, three pounds of bacon, Lucky Charms, grape juice . . . What would they choose?

I heard about this invitation to decadence after the fact, when Laurel reported on her visit. She said, "I thought of all the neat stuff we could eat, but then I remembered what you always told us."

I was greatly shocked she remembered *anything* I told them, as most daily evidence proves otherwise. "What do I always tell you?" I asked.

She cleared her throat. " 'Just because you *can* doesn't mean you *should.*' "

I said that? It sounds almost . . . profound.

Laurel noticed my stunned expression. "Don't you always say that?" she asked, as if she were afraid she got it wrong.

"Yes," I said, gathering together my mantle of authority. "I do say that. . . . So what did you have for breakfast?"

"A granola bar and cereal. Was that all right?"

"That's fine," I said. "You're a good girl." *You listened to me and you remembered!*

There is no greater compliment to a mother's ear.

Just Do It

"And this is love: that we walk in obedience to his commands."
2 John 1:6

Sometimes I wish I could hold out my arms, deepen my voice, and proclaim, "Just do it!"—and have somebody listen. It never seems to work that way. Yet I continue to try. . . .

"Just do it," I said to Emily after a lengthy discussion.

She looked at me, daring me to be logical. But there was no logical reason I wanted her to obey me. I just did. Because I was her mother. Because she was my daughter. Because it was Tuesday.

Just because.

She left the room. I slumped into the nearest chair, exhausted by our bickering, reflecting that sometimes it seemed all my waking hours were spent as a foreman, asking my kids to do something, then making sure they did it and scolding them if they did not. Why couldn't they just obey me?

"Why yes, Mother dear. I'd love to take out the garbage."
"Of course I won't watch TV until my homework's done."
"I finished filling the dishwasher, Mom. I even started it."

I shook my head, forcing my fantasies into oblivion. Did this tug-of-war happen in other families, too? Or were other parents' children obedient, hard-working and neat?

Emily popped back into the room. "All done," she said.

"You can't be. It's only been two minutes."

"It doesn't take long."

"To do a good job it does," I said. "Let's go see."

Her eyes rolled. "Don't you trust me?"

I lowered my chin and waited until her eyes met mine.

"Let me check just one more time, to make sure it's done," she said.

"Good choice."

Why couldn't they just obey me?

A voice sounded inside my head. *Why can't YOU just obey ME?*

Uh-oh. Truth time.

My children do not have a monopoly on disobedience. How many times have I failed to obey God's commands—to "just do it"? How many times has God checked over my work and found it unacceptable?

When Emily came back, I kept this in mind. I tried to be stern, yet merciful—as my Father is with me.

Love and Anger and Everything in Between

> *"Love is patient, love is kind . . . It is not rude, it is not self-seeking, it is not easily angered, it keeps no record of wrongs."*
> 1 Corinthians 13:4-5

I always start the day with the best of intentions. I vow to be in complete control of my emotions, not yielding to tears or frustration or the desire to yell at traffic lights.

This resolution lasts for approximately the time it takes me to walk from the bedroom to the kitchen. There I see that someone left the milk out all night, which means no milk for our cereal. My first angry impulse is to turn the radio on full blast. *Everybody up!* But then I realize if I get the family up now (at 5 A.M.) I will miss my designated time for reflection.

As I read the Bible, God's Word makes me feel both joyful and uncomfortable. Reading Isaiah 55:12: "The mountains and hills will burst into song before you, and all the trees of the field will clap their hands," I thrill to the wonders of God and find joy in how good he is to me. But then I read Psalm 51:9-10: "Hide your face from my sins and blot out all my iniquity. Create in me a pure heart, O God, and renew a steadfast spirit in me." That's when I realize how far I have to go.

When I hear rumbling overhead (is it thunder or my family?) I head upstairs to oversee the morning chaos.

Each of my kids greets me by pushing a different emotional button. When she was in high school, Emily would often bring on feelings of resignation—as in, I became resigned to the way she dressed. Baggy T-shirts and combat boots are not my idea of femininity, and I would tell her so, provoking occasional morning skirmishes (I think the score was Emily 23, Mom 2).

Carson is the king of procrastination. When he appears, my impatience soars, provoked by such inconsequentials as "Oh, by the way, I need black dress pants for the band concert tonight" (what band concert?) or "You have a conference with my teacher today at 10:15."

Preteen Laurel regularly raises my frustration level, since Laurel and straight answers have never been introduced. "Is your room clean?" I ask.

"Mostly."

"Which means . . . ?"

"Everything except my bed and some other stuff . . ."

When the kids tumble out the door, I take a deep breath. As a forest of gray hairs take root, I feel melancholy, a longing to call the kids back so I can wrap their childhood confusion around me. Somehow I know it can keep me warm.

The door opens and Laurel rushes in. "I forgot my science project," she says, darting past me. She hesitates at the door, backtracks and kisses me on the cheek. "Love you, Mom," she says.

Bingo, there it is, the last and most important emotion. I knew I'd get to it eventually.

Staking Your Claim

"In my Father's house are many rooms . . . I am going there to prepare a place for you." John 14:2

No matter what time I get to choir rehearsal, I can find a place to sit. That's because nobody takes my place—in the second-row altos, slightly right of center—because they are all sitting in *their* places. It's an amazing example of human nature.

I teach an editing class. It runs Thursday evenings for three weeks. Every Thursday when people return, they sit in the same seat as they did the week before. Why do they do this?

When our family sits at the dinner table or in the living room watching TV, there is no question as to who sits where. Same thing in our van. Although on long trips we do a little juggling to ease the tedium, once we've had our fill of being different, you will inevitably hear a cry of, "Time's up. Give me back my seat."

Aren't we odd creatures? So quick to stake a claim, map out our territory, grab our space. It has to do with our need to belong, to feel we have a place on the rolls of humanity. We have a chair of our own, therefore we're important—or so we imagine.

This attitude also proves how much we need the strength of God. For only he can make us feel truly at ease, at home and safe.

I find great comfort in the knowledge that God has a spot waiting for me in the next world. He's saving it just for me and I know it's mine, all mine. By believing in him I've already claimed it.

Celebrate!

> *"Give thanks in all circumstances, for this is God's will for you in Christ Jesus."* 1 Thessalonians 5:18

Carson can hit a home run. Even a grand slam. When he does, we jump up from our seats and scream as if he'd just saved the world. He's come a long way. I remember celebrating if Carson got a hit, and before that, a good swing. In the early days we celebrated if he could find his glove in time for the game. Even that earned our applause. As his achievements rose, so did our criteria for celebration.

It's the same with my writing. Now that I'm having a book published, *that* is the criterion for grand celebration. It wasn't always so. We used to go out to dinner when I'd get an article accepted—easily outspending the paycheck. Before that level of achievement, I used to celebrate a personalized rejection letter or even the fact that I finished a piece.

Even God's accomplishments are not immune to this one-upping phenomenon. We're all eager to celebrate the milestones of life: the births, the marriages, the graduations. But what about the simple accomplishments that are sprinkled throughout our days? What about celebrating a good night's sleep or the wonder of coming up with just the right words in a conversation with your boss? Or the pure ecstasy of reading a good book while cuddled on the couch on a rainy Saturday? Are those seemingly insignificant moments worth less celebration than the events that mark the culmination of many such moments? To work toward life's bigger goals is admirable, as long as we don't sacrifice the smaller moments along the way.

On the other hand, sometimes focusing on the big goals prevents us from doing anything. "I can't start reading the entire Bible I don't have time." Read a chapter a day. A page. A half-page. A verse. Remember the joy in celebrating each accomplishment, however small, until you can celebrate the larger goal.

It's unavoidable, our inclination to achieve more, leaving behind the simple successes that were our stepping stones. Yet just because we've moved on doesn't mean we can't remember and savor the sweet memories of each precious step. And jump out of our seats, scream, and applaud.

Making the Grade

*"Those who hope in the Lord will renew their strength.
They will soar on the wings like eagles;
they will run and not grow weary, they will walk and not be faint."
Isaiah 40:31*

Fact: Whether a report card is good news or bad can be determined by the exuberance or reluctance of the child bringing it home.

Eight-year-old Laurel rushed in the door, waving her report card in my face. "I got it! I got it!" No problem.

Fifteen-year-old Emily ripped open the envelope in my presence, handing me the report without looking. No problem.

Twelve-year-old Carson was notably absent. Problem.

"Carson?" I called. He appeared, head down, hands stuffed in his pockets.

"Well?" I said.

He looked up, attempting to appear innocent. "What?"

"Where's your report card?"

"Oh."

Sometimes the shortest words speak volumes. Carson dug through his backpack as if he had buried his report card three feet under. He smoothed it against his T-shirt before handing it over.

A sprinkling of Bs, a few As. Fine, fine. One C. And worse, a D.

"Most of this is great, Carson. But how could you get a C and a D?" I asked.

It turned out that Carson's C and D were the result of missing assignments and a test he had "forgotten" to study for. "We don't get Cs and Ds in this family," I proclaimed.

Carson had heard the lecture before, but as penance he resigned himself to hearing it again. He was an A student, gifted with a bright mind, and to get less than As and Bs was not fulfilling his potential. "You can do great things, Carson. But only if you do your best."

He nodded. As he went off to do anything but play the video games which were now off-limits, I heaved a motherly sigh. Our dreams for our kids aren't specific; we don't have detailed goals as to who or what they'll become. But we've always been aware of their potential. Life has so much to offer them; they have so much to offer life.

Although as adults we don't get report cards anymore, we all know we've earned a few Cs, occasional Ds, and maybe an F in the workings of our lives. We've even suffered the consequences. But God has plans for us. Big plans. Like a loving parent, he wants us to be all we can be. Mark and I won't give up on Carson, and God won't give up on us.

With his help, we'll all make the grade.

The Leading Cause of Gray Hair

> *"Pay attention and listen to the sayings of the wise;*
> *apply your heart to what I teach."*
> *Proverbs 22:17*

My husband is getting gray hair and he doesn't like it—especially when I have nary a one. Or so it seems. The truth is that Mark's hair, which is dark brown, shows more gray than mine, which is blonde.

The fact I don't outwardly show any gray hairs doesn't mean I don't feel them—inside. Actually, I have determined that the leading cause of gray hair can be traced to the utterance of a single word: *no.*

I think a study should be done to determine how many times a parent says no. Surely we could balance the federal budget if parents would pay a "no tax," perhaps a nickel, every time we said the word. I doubt the threat of taxation would stop us from saying it. The word is just too handy.

Think about it. If a mother is too tired to listen, no is a useful all-purpose response to any sentence that starts with "Can I . . ." By answering no to any can-I question you run absolutely no risk of scarring your child for life. I have yet to misplace a no. In my experience, most can-I questions have to do with personal gain. I'm still waiting to respond to such questions as, *"Can-I* give up television tonight so we can have more quality time, Mother?" or *"Can-I* please clean up my room?"

As the kids get older the can-I questions take on a different tone and the consequences of ignoring the parental no become more serious. The consequences of eating mashed potatoes with their fingers are minor compared to the consequences of drinking and driving. And so the gray hairs continue to sprout.

Sometimes, I am tempted to give in—to say yes, or even worse, to say with an exhausted sigh, "I don't care." To have them leave me alone and not argue over my no; to escape having to explain my reasons for saying the word.

But I can't. My motherly mind continues to look toward the future when they'll be on their own. Then all those no's will form a down payment on a life full of ethics, integrity and wise decisions.

Do I mind the gray hairs? Would I even object to a "no-tax"? The answer is . . . no.

Freebie Shampoos and Friendly Pillows

"But godliness with contentment is great gain." 1 Timothy 6:6

You'd never guess what my kids like about traveling. Not the chance to explore a new city. No, they're more excited by the complimentary soaps, shampoos and shoeshine cloths at the hotel. And pushing the elevator buttons. And the "free" pen and the pad of paper by the phone and the card-key that magically unlocks the door.

Our kids may now be 18, 15 and 11, but they still check out the bathroom to get dibs on the toiletries. When we were in San Diego recently, in order to prevent stampedes down the hall we had to make rules for pushing elevator buttons and unlocking the door.

Kids aren't the only ones who relish simple pleasures. Nothing is as comforting to me as my old, misshapen pillow. I can sleep anywhere as long as I'm in its company. Give Mark a bowl of plain vanilla ice cream and he is content. I can make a Hershey bar last an hour. Emily will eat macaroni and cheese hot, cold and in between. Carson craves grapes and Laurel, bananas. Simple foods for simple tastes.

Sometimes I wonder why we complicate our lives trying to give ourselves more, better, and best when we're content with far simpler and less. The apostle Paul said, "I have learned the secret of being content in any and every situation, whether well fed or hungry, whether living in plenty or in want" (Philippians 4:12). Have *we* learned to be content?

Mark and I have lived with both less and more during our married years. Our first apartment cost $75 a month. We could vacuum the entire place without moving the electrical plug. From the living room couch we had a perfect view of the toilet. Now our monthly house payments rival our salaries of years past, it takes an hour to vacuum the house, and we have five discreetly placed toilets on three floors.

Are we more content now than we were then? In some ways. But in other ways we haven't changed. I try to remember that when the kids argue about who gets the plastic shower cap. They're just enjoying life's simple pleasures. Where's my pillow?

Does Anybody Care What I Do Around Here?

> *"God is not unjust: he will not forget your work and the love you have shown him as you have helped his people and continue to help them." Hebrews 6:10*

There are some days when I feel like crying because we are out of Rice Krispies. Because the grandfather clock needs winding. Because it's rainy-sunny-hot-cold outside. There are days when I wish I lived alone in a neat two-bedroom townhome where my time was spent doing what I wanted to do, when I wanted to do it.

"Why not?" I ask myself. "Who'd notice? My family doesn't appreciate me, so why not leave them to their own devices? I'd show them."

As I sat by the townhouse pool sipping raspberry iced tea, reading a Frank Peretti novel, snacking on a box of chocolate-covered cherries (which I wouldn't have to share) I'd feel . . . no remorse whatsoever.

I'd show them how much they need me. Nobody but me knows where the 1981 tax forms are filed. Nobody but me knows which cookbook contains the pistachio dessert recipe they all love. Nobody but me has taken the time to notice which stairs creak. Without this knowledge the household would . . . would . . .

Go on without me.

All right, skip that last one. I'd show my family how much they'd miss me if I were gone. They'd miss my lopsided birthday cakes, my not-so-white laundry and my half-full cans of pop scattered around the house. They'd miss my inability to get the van parked far enough over in the garage, my habit of leaving cabinet doors open, my . . .

Oh, dear.

Maybe I'd show them how happy *I'd* be without *them*. Without Mark repeating a joke over and over, tormenting us until we finally laugh. Without Emily making me break my diet by bringing home a Peanut Buster Parfait. Without Carson making a mess of the kitchen while baking a double batch of chocolate drop cookies. Without Laurel telling me, in an absurd amount of detail, all the events of her school day. Without their voices, their laughs, their cries.

Why shouldn't I leave? Who would notice?

I would notice. And the deepest part of me, the part that thinks beyond self-gratification, knows that to be without them would be devastating.

Perhaps they *should* tell me they appreciate me more often.

But perhaps I should tell them the same.

Don't Feed the Cat from Your Plate, and Other Rules for Living

> *"Hide your face from my sins and blot out all my iniquity.*
> *Create in me a pure heart, O God,*
> *and renew a steadfast spirit within me."*
> *Psalm 51:9-10*

There are a lot of rules out there. Rules our mothers taught us that we mothers are supposed to pass on to the next generation. Here is a sampling.

There are rules for the dinner table:

1. Don't talk with your mouth full. Even if it is to tell the kids not to talk with *their* mouths full.

2. Whichever cookie you touch is yours. The temptation to do the unthinkable is powerful.

3. Don't feed the cat from your plate or she'll vomit and you'll have to clean it up. Mom didn't teach me this one. My white carpet taught me the hard way.

There are rules of hospitality:
1. Let your guests watch their favorite programs on TV. Even if it is a "Gilligan's Island" marathon.
2. Relinquish your bedroom graciously. Should I warn them that the cat likes to sleep on my side of the bed?
3. Don't check your watch and yawn. Face it, no two body clocks are ever in the same time zone. Mine is partial to whichever time zone makes it bedtime.

There are rules for being a neighbor:
1. Accept a bushel of your neighbor's zucchini with a smile. Fair is fair. I'll bring them a gallon of my newest recipe created especially for them: zucchini pudding.
2. Don't cut across your neighbor's lawn. Unless it's going through their zucchini patch.
3. Don't retrieve the morning paper wearing pink fuzzy slippers. Is it my fault their dog is afraid of my feet?

There are even rules for being a mom:
1. Don't invade a slumber party without warning. It's for my sanity as much as their dignity.

2. While driving the carpool, don't sing "Viva Las Vegas" with Elvis. Children do not appreciate fine music.

3. Don't even think of adding onions, green peppers, or anything icky to your cooking. Icky is defined as anything other than ketchup and mustard.

I accept these rules, but they don't come easy to me. They are not first or even second nature. Yet I know we're supposed to rise above our human nature and do the right thing. It's unfair, but so is the fact that cheesecake is fattening. Will I ever follow the rules without saying sarcastic asides under my breath? Will my heart ever be pure and good?

Not by my own power. There's nothing I can do but pray for strength and hope God changes me from the inside out. For only when he rules can I follow the rules with a pure heart.

Full Membership

> *"To know this love that surpasses knowledge—that you may be filled to the measure of all the fullness of God." Ephesians 3:19*

Now that our three kids are too heavy to toss over a shoulder or cuddle (they tend to squirm in both cases), we're finding other ways to enjoy our children. Laurel and I can easily overdose on figure skating and *Gone with the Wind*, while Carson and Mark can immerse themselves in baseball games (if I go, it's strictly for the hot dogs). Emily and I like to eat Mexican food at the local food court and shop, trying to outdo each other in who finds the best bargains. Each year is a new experience as we continue to discover what makes our kids tick.

Sometimes it's hard to remember what they were like when they were little. We have the requisite photos and videotapes, but the children we see in those pictures seem foreign—as do the young parents. Yet one constant theme emerges in all the pictures and memories: from the moment our kids were born, they were full-fledged members of our family.

With family membership comes responsibility. One responsibility is to be nice to each other. We give it a good shot. Yet when on occasion we snap and bark, or cut from the newspaper before everyone's read it, or accidentally eat the last brownie that was otherwise spoken for, we are (at times reluctantly) forgiven.

With family membership also come rights and honors. It is a right to always have at least one set of ears to listen to our gripes and glories. And it is an honor that at least one familial body in the audience will applaud as we play our violin, sing our solo, or hit our home run.

So it is with our spiritual lives. Once we find God, once we take that first breath of our life in him, we are full-fledged members of his family with all the rights, honors and responsibilities that go with it. Although we aren't done growing, we can never do anything to jeopardize our family standing. And, as in our earthly family, our mistakes are forgiven and our achievements are applauded.

I've always wanted to be a member of a large family. And God's got the largest brood around. Imagine the family reunion we'll have someday! As full and equal members I'll bring the brownies and you can applaud when I sing a solo—no matter how off-key it is.

Then we can truly say, "Welcome to the family."

Making a Splash

*"He repays a man for what he has done;
he brings upon him what his conduct deserves."*
Job 34:11

We have a neighborhood pool. It's one of the reasons we bought our house. Having a swimming pool within biking distance is great for the kids—and me. Their recreation gives me some much-needed breathers from their summer presence. It's not that I don't like having them around all day, twenty-four hours a day, but . . .

The fact that all three of our kids are finally old enough to go to the pool by themselves is a blessing. I don't do summer. When I used to accompany them poolside, I'd be the odd duck, sitting at a table under an umbrella, wearing shorts, a visor and sunglasses. I counted the minutes until I could be in an air-conditioned environment where I didn't perspire.

As the kids grew, their use of the pool changed. Emily makes an occasional evening visit. Laurel has to be dragged away when her skin threatens to permanently prune. And Carson . . . Carson won't go.

This last summer his refusal to participate became a real point of contention. I understood that at fifteen he might not go to the pool to "play" in the water, or even to swim. But I did think it would be a good place for him to make some new neighborhood friends. Carson would rather have hung around the house to watch TV or play video games—he thought going to the pool was too much effort. I thought a little socialized exercise was better than brain mush.

Once, Carson made up an elaborate lie about going there, even naming the time and embellishing with a few anecdotes. He forgot that little fish Laurel would be able to corroborate—or not corroborate—his story.

"Why did you lie, Carson?" I asked.

"Because I knew how much it meant to you that I go."

"Then why didn't you just go?"

That was a stumper.

The following day, Carson *promised* he'd go swimming. "If I don't go swimming today you can ground me for two months."

I shook my head, amazed. Why was he treating a privilege like a punishment?

I let him be a martyr, and with much fanfare as to his sacrifice, he went to the pool. I had the house to myself. I could get some real writing done.

But I didn't feel like it. I knew I should take advantage of the house-*sans*-kids but I found myself hedging. Maybe I'd just watch a little television, read a bit—

I stopped with the remote control in my hand. *What was I doing? Why was I treating a privilege like a punishment?*

God had given me the privilege of writing about him. Yet I was on the brink of choosing brain mush over inspiration.

I put down the remote and headed to my office. Apparently, Carson wasn't the only one who needed a push into the pool so he'd get his feet wet.

Hand me a towel.

Home But Not Alone

"Children are a reward from him." Psalm 127:3

I know why Labor Day is at the end of summer. It's the day mothers question whether the fruit of their labor pains was worth the price. Ask us the question on Memorial Day and we'll bore you with sentimental memories of our child's first tooth or our wistful tears as she trotted off to kindergarten. Ask the question on Labor Day and we'll growl, "I'll give you three for a buck ninety-eight. Will that be cash, check, or credit card?"

In September, we take an exhausted look at the rules we set in June to ensure a safe and peaceful summer—rules we revised in July and threw in the trash compactor in August. For example:

You may not go swimming until one hour after eating . . . One-half hour . . . Here, take a sandwich with you.

Come inside when the street lights turn on . . . Here's a flashlight . . . Be sure to lock up when you come in.

Summertime proves to be costly for those families where both parents work outside the home. Day-care expenses make you wonder, *Not only are the kids out of school but I have to pay money for the privilege?*

Those of us who work at home dream of daycare. It's a bit hard to concentrate when there's a trail of mildewing beach towels bisecting the house, the smell of burnt cookies wafting out of the kitchen, and the pulse of Meat Loaf (the singer, not the dinner) making me contemplate the construction of a stockade in the back yard.

I should clarify. I love my kids . . . but they make me tired. I blame The Question: "Mom, we're tired (or hungry, or bored), so what can we do now?"

So far, I have heard and attempted to answer The Question two hundred and eighty-three times. I started the summer with good intentions—and good answers. "Ask Erin over. Play school. Read a book."

But around the seventieth asking (during Day 6 of summer) my answers, and my patience, began to show signs of sanity withdrawal. "Are you sure Erin's parents don't want another child? Go pick the lock on the school. Watch 'Geraldo.' "

I answered Question #274 with a grunt. In response to Question #275, I snarled. By Question #283, my kids noticed my incisors sharpening. I never heard The Question again.

As the end of summer glows on the horizon, I realize there will be a time when I'll give anything to hear the thud of elephant feet on the stairs. I'll look back on The Question as justification of my motherly role. Guilt will sit on my shoulders until I admit my insensitivity.

But maybe not. I'll work on it.

Needs — or Wants?

*"And my God will meet all your needs
according to his glorious riches in Christ Jesus."
Philippians 4:19*

Hearing our kids say the words "I need" is a sure way to push my button. It's not that I'm unwilling to give them the necessities of life. But I have learned through long experience that their "I need" statements usually mean "I want."

For example, eleven-year-old Laurel recently stated her wish for a pair of shoes with chunky heels. "I need them," she said.

"Those are ugly," I said. "They look like the seventies."

"The seventies are back in style," she said.

I cringed. I wasn't thrilled with the seventies the first time around.

Second verse, same as the first . . .

"I need a shirt," said Carson, referring to a shirt embroidered with a specific logo. The logo was unobjectionable, but I did object to paying double the price for a T-shirt because of something that was two inches by two inches.

"With a 25-cent skein of embroidery floss and a few hours, you could sew that logo onto one of your other shirts," I said. "Besides, you don't need the shirt, you want it."

He gave me a blank look that said, *So?*

The third verse of "I need" was the most complicated. "Mom, I need to stay out until 2:30," said Emily.

"In the morning?"

"Mo-om. One of the girls at work is getting married and the wedding dance afterwards might last until—"

"Might last," I said. "Probably won't last. And even if it does, you don't have to be there."

"But Mom, I'm going off to college in the fall. I'm going to be on my own."

Don't remind me.

"I need you to trust me."

I need to trust her. I want to trust her.

As a parent my responsibility is to meet my children's needs and give into their desires as my wisdom (and patience) sees fit. It's like God does with me. With us. He doesn't promise to meet all our desires, but he will meet our needs.

I looked Emily in the eye. "You know what I *want* you to do. And you know what you *need* to do."

"What does that mean?" she asked.

"I need you to be wise."

Emily was home by 12:30. It turned out she gave me just what I needed *and* wanted that night. She was wise. And so was I.

Firing on Fort Sumter

*"Set a guard over my mouth, O LORD;
keep watch over the door of my lips."
Psalm 141:3*

Loud voices. My parental radar kicked in.

"Emily! Carson! Laurel!" I yelled. "Come down here this minute."

Three bodies appeared on the landing.

"What's going on?" I asked.

Three voices at once. Something about a calculator and one child not wanting to loan it to another. Your typical World War III escalation.

"We'll handle it," said sixteen-year-old Emily. "You stay out of it."

Me? A mother? Stay out of it?

How dare she threaten my parental right to control every situation? I told her to remember whom she was speaking to. The subsequent "discussion" went downhill faster than a car with no brakes.

But then, by some miracle, we let some sense filter into our argument.

Actually, Emily started it. In a normal voice she said, "I hate it when we yell."

"Yelling can be good," I said. "Keeping it all locked away and not talking about it is bad."

"But we're not talking."

Smart kid.

I confessed to interrupting the kids' disagreement when I had no idea what was going on, and Emily admitted she shouldn't have talked back (which to a parent is tantamount to firing on Fort Sumter). Carson relaxed. Laurel smiled.

Then we exchanged the words that are a special gift from God—the words that cleanse the soul of the hearer as well as the speaker.

"I'm sorry."

The Limits of Leashes

> *"But the fruit of the Spirit is love, joy, peace, patience, kindness, goodness, faithfulness, gentleness and self-control. Against such things there is no law." Galatians 5:22-23*

Have you ever seen those tethers some parents attach to their toddlers' arms in shopping malls? Those ropes that look like brightly-colored, coiled telephone cords? They give the child some freedom, yet keep him out of harm's way. Wishful thinking.

Some people object to these restraints, thinking they look too much like leashes. But if we're honest, we'll admit we all use leashes on our kids, although they're often invisible. It's part of our job. Yet it's wise to bear in mind that part of our children's job is to test the limits of those leashes.

It starts early. When the kids were young they took great pleasure in testing our verbal leash. They would stand by the coffee table with one arm extended toward a vase or a glass of iced tea and wait patiently until we noticed. Once we said, "No!" they toddled on to their next great leash-testing experiment.

Mark tells the story of one boyhood vacation. During this particular trip, Mark and his siblings were on the verge of global anarchy and had received many warnings from their father. Thinking they were smart (and forgetting their dad was smarter), they tried to escape to the back of the station wagon. But their father simply slammed on the brakes, causing four kids to slide toward the front, where he quelled their mutiny with a pop to their fannies. "Never think you're out of my reach," he said.

When our kids outgrow the backseat-terrorism stage, the big question becomes, Are they strong enough to set their own limits without our holding one end of the rope? Emily is now on her own in a dorm, eating, seeing, doing what she wants when she wants to do it. She's excited to be testing the leash. We're scared we've held it too tight or left too much slack.

Most likely, the truth will reveal a bit of both.

We need to trust. Sure, we've made mistakes. Our children will make mistakes. But in the end, it will be all right—as long as we never let go of the leash of love that truly binds us together.

Where Does an Overseer Go to Resign?

> *"In everything I did, I showed you that by this kind of hard work we must help the weak, remembering the words the Lord Jesus himself said, 'It is more blessed to give than to receive.' " Acts 20:35*

Mothers are jugglers—of roles. Yet there is one role I would be happy to surrender: that of an overseer.

In movies about pre-Civil War life in the South, the overseer is invariably portrayed as a ruthless meanie with a sadistic gleam in his eye. He usually carries a whip.

Except for the whip, it's an apt representation of a mother trying to get her family to hop-to. I get weary assigning chores and having to check and recheck to see if they're carried out.

"Please clean off the counters," I'll ask.

When I come back to the kitchen I'll discover they have transferred everything from the counters into the sink. I take a deep breath and clarify. "I meant you should put the dishes in the dishwasher."

"Oh," they'll say with a feigned innocence.

On my next inspection I see that the counters and sink, although cleared, are still encrusted with spaghetti sauce and grape jelly spills. I try again. "When I said clean off the counters, I meant you needed to wipe them off, too."

"Wipe them *too?*" they'll say as if I'd asked them to scrub down the Brooklyn Bridge.

It comes down to initiative. My family doesn't have it. One day, feeling sneaky—or masochistic—I put a piece of paper on the floor, in the middle of the path from the living room to the kitchen. No one passing along the much-traveled trail would be able to miss it.

They missed it.

I watched in utter fascination as they veered to the left and to the right. Laurel hopped over it. Our cat sprawled on top of it. But no one, *no one* stopped to pick it up and throw it away. When I mentioned it, the following conversation ensued.

"What paper?" they asked.

I pointed. "That paper."

"What about it?"

"Why didn't you pick it up?" I asked.

"I thought you wanted it there."

Sometimes I give up. My kids find me hiding away in the den, a dirty sock (found in the tool drawer) in one hand and three cereal bowls (found shoved under the couch) in the other hand. I stare into oblivion, my jaw slack. They whisper among themselves before venturing closer.

"Mom? Are you okay?"

One blink means yes, two means no.

They risk a hand on my pulse to see if I'm alive. "Mom, is there anything we can do?"

Hope rushes through my veins. With effort I point toward the rest of the house. "Go pick up—" My mind goes blank. "Just go."

They sigh and give me a quick peck on the cheek. Laurel stops in the doorway and says, "Mom, you're weird, but I love you anyway."

I touch my cheek. The overseer role evaporates. I'm a mother once more.

Waiting for Half-Time

> *"Do not be anxious about anything, but in everything, by prayer and petition, with thanksgiving, present your requests to God."*
> *Philippians 4:6*

I have one question: When's half-time?

Ever since our first child popped into our lives ("popped" being a relative term) I've been waiting for half-time. A time to go to the refrigerator for some food containing 327 grams of fat, a half-liter of Diet Coke to counteract the fat, and a chance to visit the bathroom for a few moments of solitude before venturing back into the game of motherhood. A chance to not think about . . . them.

With three kids who are—or will soon be—teenagers, I'm still waiting.

When you have a newborn in the house, he or she can be left alone only for short periods of time. Even if you do sneak to a quiet corner while the baby naps, it's not a proper half-time because your mind is consumed with worry. Should the baby be on her stomach or back? Is the room too warm or too drafty? Did that last burp really count or will the little darling spit up all over the freshly laundered sheet?

When your child is a toddler, you can't leave the room because he won't let you. Your docile baby has turned into a rambunctious puppy dog who follows at your heels—and occasionally under them. This is the point in your life when you wonder if you'll ever enter a bathroom alone—for their duty or yours.

When your kids are in school, you can't enjoy half-time because you're never home. You pay bills, read books and eat lunch in the driver's seat while waiting to pick them up. The local gas station has days in your honor and the high point of your life is finding shortcuts to Scouts or gymnastics class.

When your children start driving and/or dating, you may think you're ready for half-time, only to find you're too nervous to enjoy it. Will they be strong and resist temptation? No and probably no. In the free time you do have, you pray. A lot.

And after the kids are grown? Well . . . my mother still calls to see how my sore throat is doing, to remind me to bring an umbrella to my kids' ball games, and to share a new recipe that is especially healthy (hence foreign to my taste buds).

God meant for mothering to be an all-time job. We'd better accept that fact. I guess if he doesn't get a break, neither should we.

A Sense of My Mother

"Her children arise and call her blessed;
her husband also, and he praises her:
'Many women do noble things,
but you surpass them all.'"
Proverbs 31:28-29

Whenever I smell the perfume White Shoulders I think of my mother. It was her dress-up scent. She would emerge from the master bedroom wearing a hand-sewn, designer-quality dress, her hair in a French roll. She would lean down to kiss me good-bye and I would smell that luscious floral. When I was in college I bought a bottle of White Shoulders for myself, but it was never my scent. It was—and is—hers.

I can still see our kitchen table. Every morning before school, we'd answer Mom's call of "Breakfast!" and find the table set, waiting for us. If it was spring, there would be a vase of iris or grape hyacinths in the middle of the table. If it was winter the flowers were replaced with pine cones and sprigs of pine needles. Breakfast together was a constant in our lives.

So was homemade bread. Mom did it the pre-bread machine way, kneading the dough, letting it rise in a stainless steel pan with a cotton towel over the top, capturing the heat from a floor register. We would toast a slice of fresh bread and slather it with butter until it was heavy with taste.

I still love hearing my mother's voice—although my husband could do with hearing it a little later in the day. If the phone rings between seven and seven-thirty in the morning, he's learned to let me answer it. Mom knows I'm up, and have been for hours—after all, I take after her. We talk to each other a couple of times a week. The words aren't significant, but the need for connection is.

Finally, touch. A mother's touch has healing powers. As a child I was susceptible to stomach flu, yet each time I rushed to the bathroom, Mom would be close behind. She'd stand behind me, her hand placed over my forehead, giving me strength and hope.

Two years ago, my mother needed my comforting touch. When she was in the hospital, having undergone major surgery, I stood by her bed and held her hand. It was then I marveled at how frail it seemed, so soft and insubstantial, like air. If only my hand could heal like hers had healed.

What memories will my children have of me? What sights, sounds and scents will they cherish?

I have much to live up to.

For Worse—and for Better

> *"I will betroth you to me forever;*
> *I will betroth you in righteousness and justice,*
> *in love and compassion.*
> *I will betroth you in faithfulness*
> *and you will acknowledge the LORD."*
> *Hosea 2:19*

My husband and I are as different as Broadway and baseball, devil's food and angel food. Sometimes, in weak moments—or angry moments—I wonder why we ever married.

It's not that I would truly consider being apart, as I feel disdain for both the D-words: death and divorce. But when Mark really aggravates me, when the mere sight of him makes my blood boil, our differences take on cosmic proportions and the traits we share seem inconsequential.

After twenty-one years of marriage I've visited every emotion known to woman. Love, hate, remorse, frustration, disgust, hope, fear . . . I've dabbled in them all, often within minutes of each other. Yet I wouldn't trade one of these emotions for all the chocolate chips in China. Here's why.

Fear: I'm a stubborn woman. I know how to set my feet, dig in, and push. There are times when I've nearly pushed too far, finding a fiendish pleasure in "winning" an argument. I've felt the fear that follows such an argument: fear that I'd lose him, fear that the pieces of our marriage couldn't be put together again. But the fear serves a purpose: it wakes me up and sends me to my knees.

Hope: What would we do without it? Looking to the past gives me the most hope. Remembering all we've been through—intellectually, financially, emotionally, spiritually. We're not the same people we were when we got married. We're better individuals and we're better as a couple—which means that twenty years hence we'll be even better than we are now.

Disgust: I'm disgusted by the way we argue. We are opposite in our tactics. I blurt things out, often saying what I shouldn't say. Then I'm ready to make up. Mark stews. Over days. Adding along the way an assortment of diced grudges, chopped transgressions and minced feelings. Only through practice (I never did like to practice) have we come to recognize this—and deal with it.

Frustration: If only he'd see things my way! It's so obvious I'm right. Sometimes. Once in awhile. Seen a blue moon lately? I used to pray that God would make Mark see my side of things, thereby making arguing obsolete. It took a few years for me to realize that God wasn't necessarily on my side; Mark was right once in awhile. Now *that's* frustrating.

Remorse: Until remorse waves its white flag, an argument is doomed to rise perpetually like an escalator at the mall. I'll admit—with a proper level of pride—that I am always the first to feel this blessed emotion. That's because I'm done arguing while Mark's still getting started. I've learned the benefits of a sincere "I'm sorry," even if it's not accepted right away. It's a balm on the infection of anger.

Hate: I've done it. I've hated him. Deep down, get-out-of-my-sight hate. And it scares me. It makes me groan, it makes me cry. It makes me pray. Hard. Hate is the emotion I hate. It is a totally selfish emotion. Hate is the enemy of marriage.

Love: When I was an unmarried teenager and my sister, Crys, was an old married pro with five years under her belt, she told me she loved her husband differently than she did as a newlywed. "We're friends." At the time, I thought that seemed like a step in the wrong direction. Only now do I realize how much additional love is required to be friends than to be merely lovers. After twenty-one years, it is my husband's friendship I cherish the most.

And, in happy moments, I *know* why we got married. Because I am for him and he is for me. And God is behind us both.

Worth the Wait

"I waited patiently for for the L<small>ORD</small>;
he turned to me and heard my cry."
Psalm 40:1

If patience is a virtue, I am doomed.

I try to smile as I stand in line at the grocery store while a lady digs through 4,215 coupons to save 20 cents on Malt-O-Meal. I try to keep my palm away from the horn of my car as the man in front of me combs his hair through a green light. And I try to be patient as God doles out my dreams on his schedule instead of mine.

I have a lot to do. Friends to see, stories to write, dishes to wash. If the world would run on my schedule there would be no problem. I'd have my own personal checker at the grocery store and a designated lane on my favorite streets so I could zip along without obstacles slowing me down. And I'd hand God a schedule of when my dreams should be answered so as not to interfere with "Oprah" or Carson's dentist appointments.

Unfortunately, I am nearly certain—all right, I'm positive—God is going to ignore my requests. Too self-centered and all that. Fine. I'll accept his refusal concerning my groceries and drive time. But what about the rest? When *is* God going to answer my prayers—the deep-down ones I dream about?

There's got to be a secret way to obtain The Answer. Such as . . .

1. Pray without ceasing. Maybe if God gets tired of hearing it, he'll give in (it works for my kids). I give it a shot. I repeat my mantra until my mind turns to Jell-O. No answer.

2. Logic. I take out my date book and ask God to consider next Friday. It's my husband's birthday and the answer to my prayers would be the perfect gift. No answer.

3. How about a deal? If I can give God one perfect day, a day where I am a gracious wife-mother-accountant-writer-maid-cook-chauffeur-friend, God will reward me.

My good intentions last until 7:05 A.M., when my daughter informs me she needs a red three-ring notebook for her first-period class or she'll get a D. No answer.

4. The subtle approach. *Hey, this is no big deal, God. You know what I'd like but if you can't swing it, life goes on.* No answer.

5. Visualization. I can see it! I have pretend conversations with people vital to my dream. I plan what I will wear (my taupe suit with the embroidery on the jacket). My imagined joy brings tears. No answer.

6. Finding the "signs." Like a detective collecting clues, I take the receipt of a letter on a certain day, plus the appearance of two articles about my dream, plus the fact I lost three pounds to mean it's going to happen today! Everything's falling into place. It's perfect! No answer.

7. Doubt. Maybe my dream isn't God's will. I pray it is. No answer.

At this point, I nearly give up. But somehow, I don't. I can't.

Okay, God, if you want me to learn patience, just wait! I'll be the most patient, long-

suffering lamb you have ever seen. I will not give up. I'll continue to pray. You want patience? You want faith? You want persistence? You got it!

Then one day, it happens. I'm in the middle of folding the laundry, wearing my grungiest sweatsuit, my mind full of the pick-ups, should-dos and better-hurries of the day.

God hands me my dream. Unexpected. Unplanned. Unannounced. The purest gift.

I thank God . . . I thank God . . . I thank God . . . *This mantra is easy.*

Will I ever be impatient again? It's guaranteed. Is there a secret to making prayers—and dreams—come true? Yes, there is. Faith. And a lot of patience. But the best part?

His gifts are worth the wait.

Have I Flunked Parenting 101?

"Be joyful in hope, patient in affliction, faithful in prayer."
Romans 12:12

Had I blown it as a parent?

When Emily went away to college, I was excited for her and helped her move onto campus with barely a regret. I realized it was time for her to move on. I would let her go graciously, without a fuss.

I had my fears. For her safety, her purity, her self-control. Although we'd taught her well, these fears were based on Emily's attitude that she was invincible and knew everything.

"Don't worry, Mom. Trust me."

I'd give it a try.

When we called to see how her first day of school went, Emily divulged that she had missed the first class of her college life. She overslept. Why did she oversleep? She'd been up late the night before. And the night before that. And . . .

It seems Emily, who had induced little parental worry in high school, had discovered the wonders of partying.

"Take it down a notch, Emily," I told her.

"I'm fine," she assured me. "Last night we went to a frat party—"

My spine tingled at the words. "Frat party? Oh, Emily, you have to be really careful at frat parties. They were wild when we went to school. I hate to think what they're like now."

"I went with a bunch of guys, Mom. They protected me."

"Guys? As in 'people' or 'boys'?"

"Boys, Mom." She sighed. "I haven't met many girls yet."

"What were they protecting you *from?*"

She hesitated. She didn't want to admit that my fears were valid. "Just stuff in general, Mom. They walked me home."

Was it possible gentlemen still existed on college campuses?

"Got to go, Mom. We have some people coming over."

"But it's 10:30. You have class tomorrow."

"Not until nine. Don't worry so much, Mom."

I hung up, smothered with a feeling of failure. Where had we gone wrong? Why was Emily acting as if moving away from home was the equivalent of being released from prison?

"At least she's talking to us," Mark said. "At least she's not hiding what she's doing."

A part of me wished she'd keep it to herself. It would make my feelings of failure less biting.

"But what if she makes a mistake?" I asked him.

"She'll have to deal with it. We'll all have to deal with it. We've done our best; we have to let her go."

I nodded, knowing that doubt and failure are a part of life.

But so are forgiveness and love.

Being "Gifted"

"Each man should give what he has decided in his heart to give, not reluctantly or under compulsion, for God loves a cheerful giver."
2 Corinthians 9:7

Last Mother's Day I looked at my husband expectantly. He pretended not to notice. I cleared my throat, implying, "Where's my present?"

Mark grinned and said what he says every Mother's Day: "I gave the kids five dollars to get you something. It's not my fault they didn't do anything with it."

It's a running gag that has been going on for eighteen years. The fact is, Mark doesn't buy me Mother's Day presents. He takes me out to dinner or brunch, but I've never had an actual box to open. It's not that I really care, but . . . I really care.

To be fair, since my kids have become old enough to see through their dad's "joke," they've come up with presents with or without his mythical five dollars. Coupons for chores, pots of geraniums made in Sunday school and mugs adorned with cute sayings. I have enough mugs to kaffee-klatsch with most of the mothers west of the Mississippi.

As children get old enough to spend their own money, gift-giving moves into the I-got-it-on-sale phase. One Christmas, Emily was fairly bursting to have me open the gift from her. Inside was a battery-operated nail polish dryer. I decided not to mention that I don't wear nail polish. Emily beamed at my thanks. "I thought you'd like it. I got it on sale."

I can't complain. She learned it from me.

My siblings and I bought our parents an electric can opener once. In 1967 it was a new invention and we thought it was cool. Especially since it was avocado, and even if it was for their silver wedding anniversary. Then there was the gift that I, and I alone, gave to my grandparents for their fiftieth anniversary. It was an earthen pot holding six velvet-covered stems, each topped with an orange and yellow burlap "flower" coaster. I still cringe when I see pictures of the gift table with my contribution standing out like Li'l Abner at a debutante ball.

My parents and grandparents never let on that our gifts might have contained more innovation than taste. They knew, as I've learned, that things, even expensive things, don't last. Memories of a bouquet of dandelions—or even a bouquet of burlap—outlast all the rest.

The Habits of Halfway

> *"Never be lacking in zeal, but keep your spiritual fervor, serving the Lord."* Romans 12:11

When I eat, I do it all the way. Fettuccine Alfredo, a fresh green salad with black olives and sweet red onions, garlic bread, and a cannoli stuffed with whipped cream. *Bene!*

But such perfection demands a price: exercising.

So I walk. I put on my guilt, my shoes and my headphones and head off on my quest to burn calories.

The other day as I walked, Twila Paris sang "Joy of the Lord" in my ears. My feet fell into rhythm with her song of glory. I raised my arms from their normal, easy swing, crooked my elbows, and started them pumping at my sides.

Hey, this is great. Moving my arms like this makes me feel like I'm really doing some good.

But such extra effort was tiring. I felt a bead of sweat threaten my brow. Instinctively, I slowed down. A nice stroll was one thing but this sweat business was another. I fell into my ordinary pace—and felt my enthusiasm die along with my speed.

No wonder I hadn't lost weight. I was exercising only halfway. Half—

I stopped in my tracks, making a neighbor's cat arch her back and hiss at me. What other things in my life were done halfway? What other things weren't producing the maximum fruit because I didn't want to push past the quick and easy and venture into real work and real commitment? My family life? My work? My spiritual walk . . .

Walk. Spiritual walk.

I flinched at the truth. The cat darted away.

Things had to change. Now.

I moved forward, accelerating, forcing my arms to pump at my side. One block, two . . . My mind wandered. With disgust I found that my arms had returned to the modest swing of past walks. Obviously, it would take concentrated work to make extra effort second nature.

With renewed determination, I bent my elbows and made my arms move. Pump. Pump. I vowed to give my best to everything I did: my exercising, my family, my work, my God.

Please, God. I want to make my efforts count. Give me some of your strength to keep me from slipping back to the easy way.

As I turned the last corner toward home, I felt stronger. It wasn't me against myself anymore, valiantly—but vainly—fighting the habits of halfway. I had God to help me. And I knew he'd be with me—all the way.

Growing Up Gracefully

"But just as you excel in everything—in faith, in speech, in knowledge, in complete earnestness and in your love for us—see that you also excel in this grace of giving." 2 Corinthians 8:7

When did I grow up?

Emily went off to college this year. The last thing I remember, *I* was the one going off to college.

When I was in college, the world revolved around my goals, my schedule and my happiness. I wanted to get a degree in architecture, get married, be on my own. I went after those dreams with the faith of youth that they would come true. And they did.

I remember someone whose life had not been as rosy as mine snapping at me, "Why do you and Mark act like you're happy all the time? I have one good day a month." It was a shocking revelation. We had one *bad* day a month. Of course, I didn't let this person's dim view of life drag me down. I knew that if you expected bad things to happen, they would, and if you expected good things to happen . . .

And they did. Mark and I graduated with those degrees in architecture. We built a string of houses whose size corresponded to the growing size of our family. We started a business. I happily accepted the role of a young mother with three kids nipping at my heels. They didn't slow me down. If I wanted to go shopping, they sat near a rack of blouses reading books and coloring. If I wanted to be in a play at the community theatre, I was.

When Emily became a teenager, I assumed the new role with the knowledge that I would be a good mom-to-a-teen because it hadn't been *that* long since I'd been a teenager myself. If our lives got more complicated with various teen activities, not to worry. I could fit them in around my newest goal to be a writer.

But when all three of my kids hit the double digits, when I turned forty, I realized other people did not see me as young anymore. Emily was the young woman. I was . . . a grown-up.

But I hadn't grown up. Not yet.

Then Emily was gone. All those years preparing her were a flash. A blink. I panicked as I tried to remember her as a baby in my arms. A toddler learning to walk. The memory of her first day of school—or was it Carson's? I had been so busy. . . . Had I been too busy to be the kind of mother I should have been? Could have been?

With shame I realized that part of me was still a kid who thought the world revolved around her needs. What had I missed by fitting the kids into my schedule? What had they missed because I had "played the part" of a mom, giving them only a *part* of me?

I was never a bad mother. But neither was I a great mother. I was so caught up in hoarding my "good days" *for* myself that I didn't give enough *of* myself.

Thankfully, there's still time. I've learned that love is more than an emotion; it is an action.

When did I finally grow up? When I learned how to give.